Haikus for Life:

Live, Love and Laugh With Passion!

Steven A. Yagyagan

ISBN-13: **978-1481230650** (CreateSpace-Assigned)
ISBN-10: **1481230654**
BISAC: Poetry / Asian / Japanese

First Printing (Vol. 1, 1st edition), February 7, 2013

ISBN-13: **978-0615771847** (Steven A. Yagyagan)
ISBN-10: **061577184X**
BISAC: Poetry / Asian / Japanese

Second printing (Vol. 1, 2nd edition), February 27, 2013

Greeting cards were created by Regina B. Yagyagan
Photographs by Steven A. Yagyagan, Regina B. Yagyagan,
            Marvin R. Vistro, Helen C. Vistro
            Photography By Jim (Waialua, HI) of
            graduation photo of Robert A. Pabro, Jr.

Designed by Steven A. Yagyagan
Prepared by Steven A. Yagyagan

Published by:
Steven A. Yagyagan
Chula Vista, CA
e-mail: plantationprince@gmail.com
Website: www.princeoftheplantation.blogspot.com
Facebook: www.facebook.com/pages/steven-a-yagyagan-author/poet

Publishing services by:
CreateSpace, an Amazon Company
4900 LaCross Road
North Charleston, SC 29406

Printed in the United States of America

2

Introduction

In the summer of 2011, I celebrated my fiftieth birthday and I started to come to grips with my sister Fausta's passing two years earlier. At fifty, I felt I needed to get back into shape again. So, I started running once again on the 4th of July.

I pushed myself to run seven days a week. On July 31st, I began to notice and appreciate Mother Nature's beauty, which prompted me to look deep within my soul. I began to feel my spirit renewed again.

Every little detail caught my eyes, ears and nose. The colorful hues of greens and browns, the brilliant rays of light, the still morning dew, the birds chirping and the sweet floral scents that permeate the air captivated me. I also started to rekindle my love for haiku. So, I began to feel the words come to me naturally in haiku form. I could hear the words being read aloud in my head as each syllable unfolded. Ahh, the sights, sounds and smells tickle my senses.

As the days passed, I longed to see more of Mother Nature. Day after day, I anxiously awaited the next day and the next day and the next day to arrive so I could be intimate with her again. Little-by-little, I expanded my running route. From 2 miles, I went to 8 miles a day, 7 days a week. I did this for nearly six months straight, rain or shine.

A love fest ensued. I couldn't get enough of the exhilaration of my morning run and the beauty of the trees, the grassy knolls, the hills, the birds, the waves, the wind rustling in the trees, the brilliant rays of light, the children playing and laughing. I began relating the beauty of nature to human life. I started to take photos to help me illustrate the meaning behind the words.

Here we are in February 2013 and I'm still writing haikus religiously, daily. I even began to write limericks. Limericks are so much fun. I'll share some with you in my next book, Haikus For Life, Volume 2. My haikus and my life have evolved spiritually these past two years.

I've bent the rules a little on haikus. Tradition haikus use a 5-7-5 syllable format. I use 4-6-4 and 6-8-6 in some of my poems. My goal of this book is to share my beautiful journey with others who might seek inspiration, encouragement and motivation. You'll get a sense of the highs and lows in my life at that moment. Initially, I wrote background information on each poem. I decided to remove the majority of the information so that you could interpret them and apply them to your own life. I did leave the dates and times I wrote each poem as a reminder of when each poem was written. All of the photos were taken by me, my wife and possibly some of our friends.

Whatever challenges you face in life, I hope my haikus and photos help you in your journey. I hope my poems allow you to live a life of love, laughter and passion for who you love, you inclusive, and what you enjoy doing every breathing moment of your special and beautiful life.

Thank you for reading my book. I welcome your feedback via e-mail: plantationprince@gmail.com. Visit my blog: www.PrinceofthePlantation.blogspot.com for updates.

Aloha!
Steve

Acknowledgements

This is the first of three books I have lined up for publishing this year. In my journey, I have so many people who have "been there" for me and for my family. The road hasn't been easy but their tireless support, their grace, and their immeasurable and boundless love have been so instrumental to my success. I take full responsibility for any flaws overlooked in this book but I share all the praise and success with every one of them. For my wife Regina and our children, Matthew and Gabrielle, I love you so much! It is to them that I dedicate this book.

Kay Yamada
Roland Padua
Jowette Padua
Helen C. Vistro
Jessebel Cellery
Jesse G. Medina
Marvin R. Vistro
Cora M. Ordonio
Dale J. Bangalan
Jose O. Bangalan
Robert Allen Pabro
Rose Maria Woods
Sipepa Faitau Faga
Marie Arucan Bilan
Erlinda Y. Arconado
Pio Ibanez Yagyagan
Heather Tauvela Myles
Miriama Tauvela Faitau
Fausta Clara Ann Manners
Gabrielle Nohelani Yagyagan
Matthew Joseph-Keoni Yagyagan
Regina Bangalan Yagyagan
God's Divine Mercy

Still of the morning,
The sun peeks through the gray clouds,
Cool breeze brings me peace

Sunday, July 31, 2011 @ 5:33 am

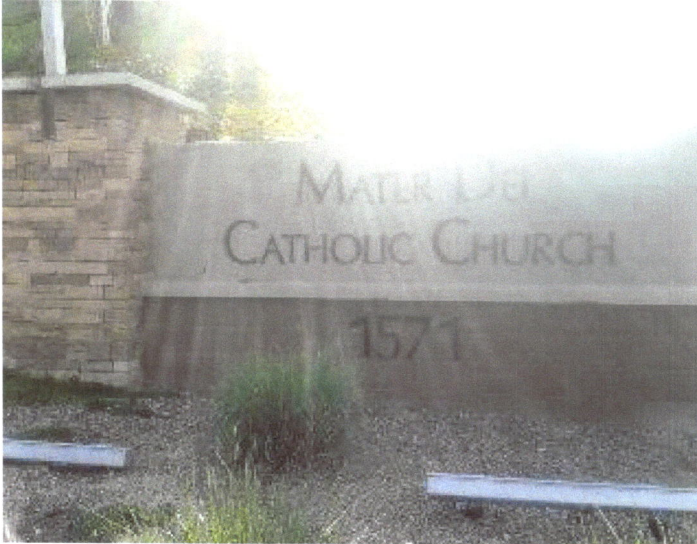

Sunrise from the East
Shadows cast along the trail
Burst of energy

Monday, August 1, 2011 @ 7:17 am

Solar rays at dawn,
Green grass shimmering with dew,
Kissed by the crisp air

Wednesday, August 3, 2012 @ 7:26 am

A life of passion,
Swirling winds seize the moment,
Boundless joy, love, peace

Saturday, August 20, 2011 @ 8:43 am

Quietly, they sit,
Waiting for the wind's tickle
Birds sit in their arms

Friday, Aug. 5, 2011 @ 7:23 am

Rubber on asphalt,
Like the sound of waves crashing,
Soothes my peaceful soul

Monday, August 8, 2012 7:47 am

Her heart, full of love,
Faith in God, selfless, giving,
Bringing friends closer

Tuesday, August 9, 2011 12:12 am

We lay her to rest,
Let her soul rise up again.
We love you, Marie

Friday, August 19, 2011 @ 7:59 am

Though scattered apart,
No ocean, no land too wide,
Our lifeblood is strong

Thursday, August 11, 2011 @ 8:23 am

Family is blood,
Friends become your family,
Filling hearts with joy

Sunday, August 14, 2011 @ 8:50 am

Blink, life flies by you,
Live each moment with passion,
Live life with meaning

Saturday, August 13, 2011 @ 8:54 am

My brother for life,
Your love, unconditional,
'Til we meet again

Thursday, October 27, 2011 @ 12:34 am

Life ends, soul lives on,
Quietly, our soul departs,
Eternal journey

(Photo credit: Photography by Jim, Waialua, HI)
Monday, August 15, 2011 @ 8:08 pm

Determined runner,
He pushes, step after step,
Dripping beads of sweat

Wednesday, August 10, 2011 @ 7:44 am

Morning air is crisp
Rays of the sun warm my soul
Alone, not lonely

Sunday, August 21, 2011 @ 8:08 am

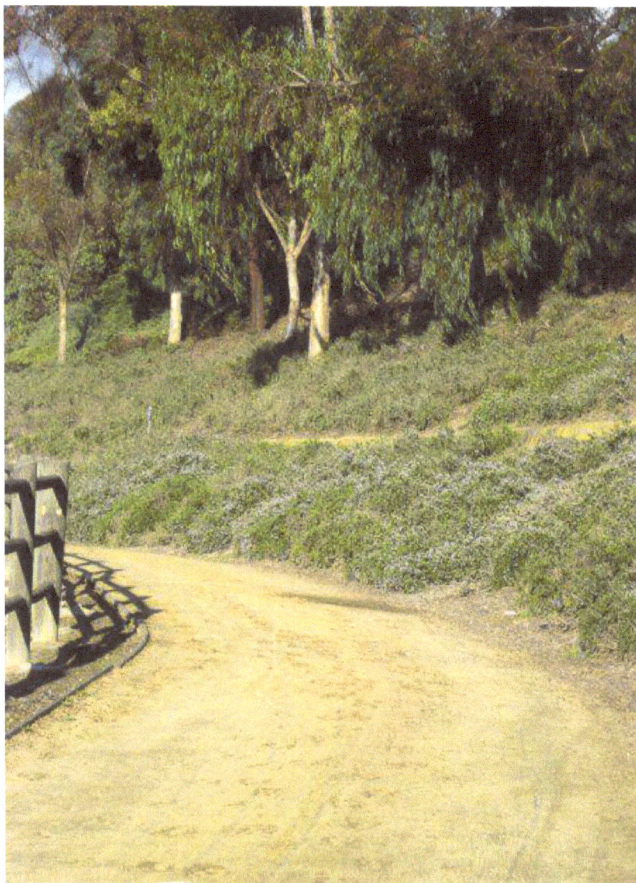

Draped with greenery
Beautiful, top to bottom
Sloping elegance

Tuesday, August 25, 2011 @ 8:56 am

Little waves lapping,
Tsunami of cars ahead,
Peaceful uphill run

Thursday, September 1, 2011 @ 8:11 am

Peace, tranquility,
Pacing, breathing, clearing mind
Wind kisses my skin

Tuesday, September 13, 2011 @ 6:36 am

Parents age with time
Flowers bloom, age gracefully
Love and care for them

Friday, August 26, 2011 @ 6:42 am

Your love is boundless
Forgiving, overflowing
Thankful for your love

For my wife, Regina, on our wedding anniversary.
Saturday, August 27, 2011 @ 1:16 am

Your love is patient
Your love is kind and gentle
Your love is my love

Tuesday, August 30, 2011 @ 8:58 am

Secured by your love
Securing you with my love
Until our last days

Wednesday, August 31, 2011 @ 8:34 am

Her heart has my heart,
Her soul more than her body,
She's simply awesome

Friday, September 30, 2011 @ 7:59 am

I can own my love,
Is marriage like ownership?
Can I own your love?

Saturday, September 10, 2011 @ 12:50 am

Even when it hurts,
Should we limit love?
Love is unconditional

Wednesday, September 7, 2011 @ 7:38 am

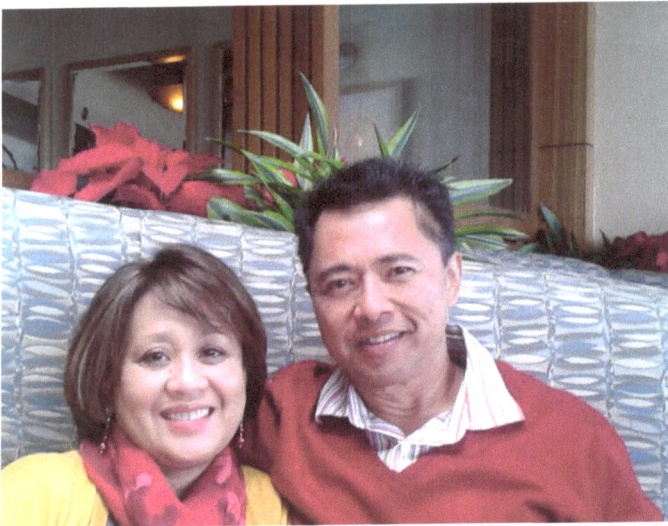

We're lovers and friends
Years of loving, nurturing
Love is a lifetime

Thursday, September 8, 2011 @ 8:04 am

Friends and relations
Caring, trusting, and loving
Extraordinary

Sunday, August 28, 2011 @ 5:44 pm

Faith, hope, love guide us
Faith gives strength, hope to survive
Love, strongest of all

Monday, August 29, 2011 @ 7:07 am

Your life's challenges
Hopefully leads to lessons
A brighter future

Friday, September 2, 2011 @ 12:00 am

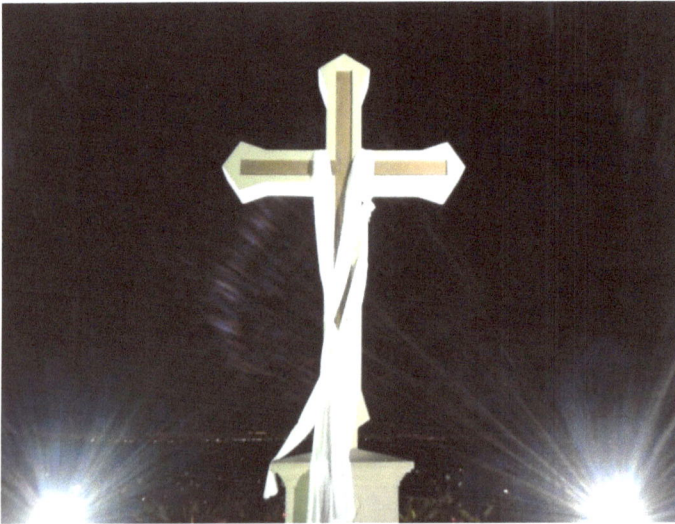

Seasons come and go
Relationships come and go
Life comes...and then goes

Saturday, September 23, 2011 @ 8:29 am

Face demons head on,
Relinquish anxieties,
Accept and move on

Friday, September 2, 2011 @ 12:00 am

Yin and Yang of love
Deeper than just, "I love you!"
Caring and sharing

Sunday, September 4, 2011 @ 12:41 am

Eyes tell the story,
A smirk, a smile says a lot,
The heart never lies

Tuesday, Sept. 6, 2011 @ 11:13 pm

The comforts of life
Electrical dependence
Live a simple life

Friday, September 9, 2011 @ 9:48 pm

Crisis can show truth
Calm, leadership, character
Bring forth solutions

Friday, September 9, 2011 @ 9:48 pm

For some, love is plain
For me, love is much deeper
All encompassing

Saturday, September 10, 2011 @ 12:50 am

Hide under the skin,
Catches up with everyone,
Let the truth be told

Sunday, September 11, 2011 @ 5:55 am

Precious human life,
Many lost in senseless wars,
Everlasting peace

Sunday, September 11, 2011 @ 5:55 am

Good friends can hurt you,
Forgive and lighten your heart,
Feel the weight lifted

Monday, September 12, 2011 @ 5:12 am

Time can heal your mind,
Focus on beauty and peace,
Appreciate life

Wednesday, September 14, 2011 @ 1:07 am

Breathe the crisp, clean air,
Enjoy the orange sunset,
Ahhh, rays of the sun

Wednesday, September 14, 2011 @ 1:07 am

Slow life down, heal soul,
Seagulls, shore breaks, salt mist air,
Sink your feet in sand

Wednesday, September 14, 2011 @ 1:07 am

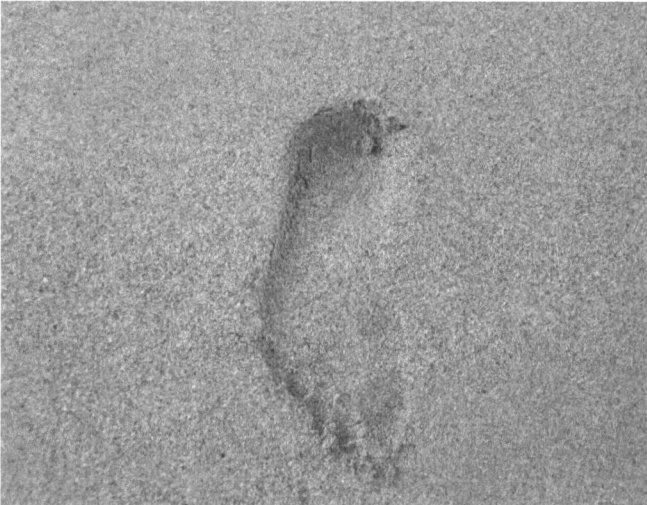

Flesh versus spirit,
Soul connection transmits love,
Meaning and purpose

Thursday, September 15, 2011 @ 3:31 am

A passion for life,
Passionate for all I do,
Passionate for you

Friday, September 16, 2011 @ 7:49 am

In the midst of friends,
Fun times, much respect and love,
Memories for life

Saturday, September 17, 2011 @ 8:46 am

Some can criticize,
Humility is a choice,
Enlighten yourself

Tuesday, September 20, 2011 @ 11:49 pm

Run for endorphins,
Feeling young, energetic,
A natural high

Wednesday, September 21, 2011 @ 9:59 pm

Early morning mist,
Gently landing on my face,
Peaceful, leisure run

Saturday, September 24, 2011 @ 7:51 am

Ho'omakaukau,
Every stroke pulls the va'a,
Me and the ocean

(Ho'omakaukau:"get ready" in Hawaiian. Va'a is a canoe)
Sunday, September 25, 2011 @ 6:03 am

Forks in trail of life,
You've got to follow your road,
Make wise decisions

Monday, September 26, 2011 @ 7:27 am

A dog is loyal,
Keeping pace with his master,
Guards him from strangers

Tuesday, September 27, 2011 @ 7:27 am

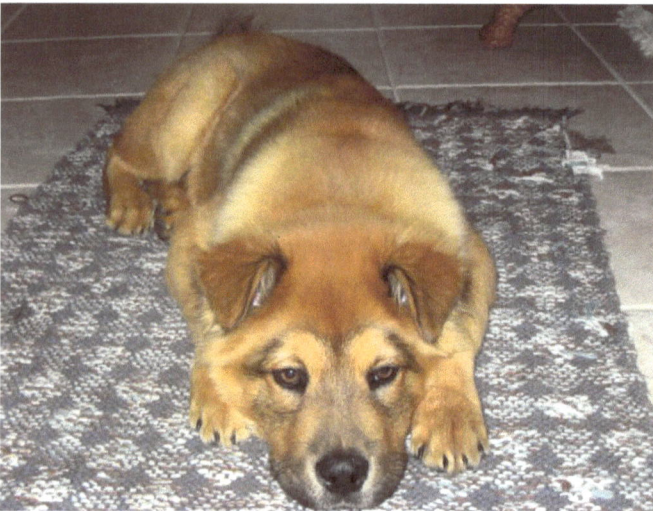

Early in the dawn,
Runners, walkers come and go,
Each at their own pace

Wednesday, September 28, 2011 @ 7:00 am

Protects his master,
On guard, sniffing out trouble,
Koa's a good dog

Friday, October 21, 2011 @ 11:53 am

Feel the vibrations,
Blending our diverse talents,
Beautiful music

A haiku for my friends in Da 2nd Wind Band
who LOVE to share their diverse musical talents,
harmonizing and blending beautiful music.

Thursday, September 29, 2011 @ 7:30 am

Passionate people,
Special people in our lives,
Love, care, and patience

Thursday, October 20, 2011 @ 11:12 am

Be thankful for friends,
Support and respect your friends,
Friends are family

Monday, October 3, 2011 @ 10:38 am

Let go of your pain,
Forgiveness lightens your load,
Fill your heart with joy

Monday, October 3, 2011 @ 10:38 am

Show love to your spouse,
Subtle touches say a lot,
Kiss them and hug them

Monday, October 3, 2011 @ 10:38 am

Don't be complacent,
Time does not stand still for us,
Put meaning in life

Tuesday, October 4, 2011 @ 7:41 am

Thankful for good friends,
Supporting loving fam'ly,
Feel God's strength within

Wednesday, October 5, 2011 @ 1:42 pm

You're my gift from God,
Protecting and loving me,
Your strength comes from Him

Thursday, October 6, 2011 @ 7:02 am

Run trails or circles,
How do you handle life's curves?
My friend, stay the course

Friday, October 7, 2011 @ 2:33 pm

Spirit of squirrel,
Working together as one,
Make good things happen

Monday, October 10, 2011 @ 8:14 am

The invitation
Ev'rything we do matters
Ev'ry moment counts

Monday, October 10, 2011 @ 8:14 am

You're a special friend
I remember all you've done
Legacy lives on

Monday, October 10, 2011 @ 8:14 am

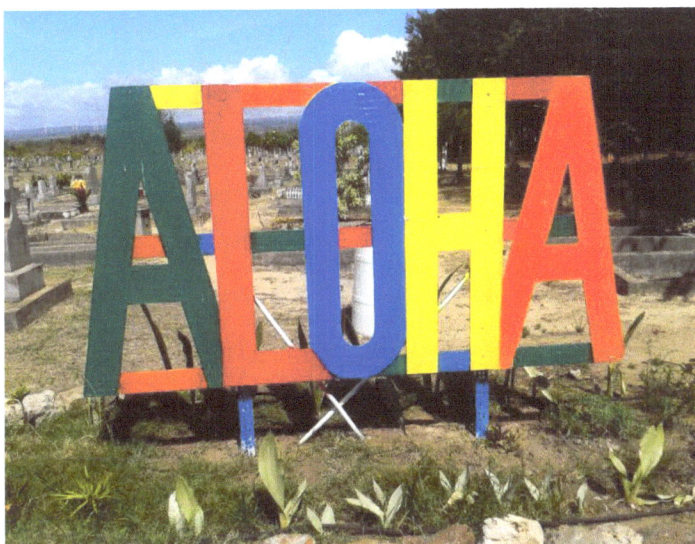

Met my new aiga,
It's nice ta, nice ta know ya,'
Let's do it again

(Aiga: "Family" in Samoan)
Wednesday, October 12, 2011 @ 8:43 am

I am my challenge,
Keeping my head in the game,
Gotta tough it out

Wednesday, October 12, 2011 @ 8:43 am

Drivers rush to work,
Quietly, the trees watch them,
He's at peace running

Thursday, December 15, 2011 @ 8:13 AM

My heart weighs heavy,
I know I need to go on,
I want to be strong

Thursday, October 13, 2011 @ 8:33 am

Giving all of me,
Ribs, shoulder, jaws and heart hurts,
A slow painful death

Friday, October 14, 2011 @ 9:23 pm

His heart writhes in pain,
Difficult to love again,
Deeply, he spirals

Saturday, October 15, 2011 @ 7:39 am

High testosterone,
Egos let them lose control,
They fight to the end

Friday, December 16, 2011 @ 8:22 AM

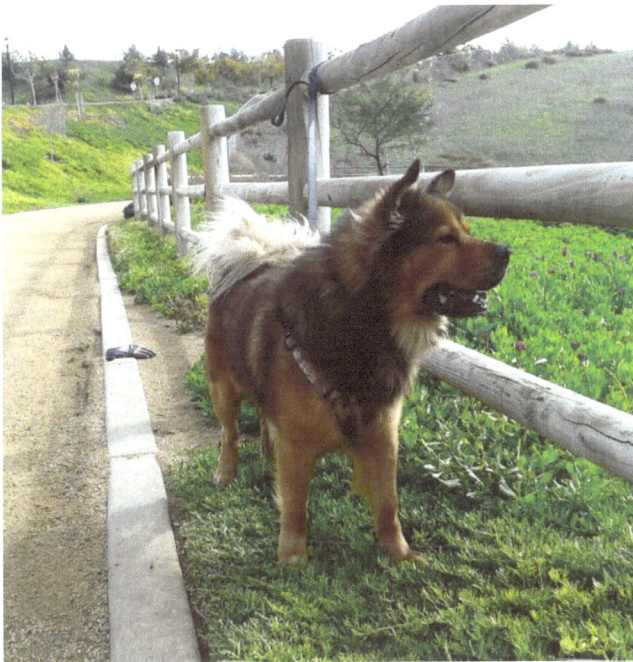

Jealousy and rage,
Jealousy is not mature,
Only love conquers

Friday, December 30, 2011 @ 7:13 AM

Feelings are tricky,
Do you show'em or hold'em?
Others, defensive

Thursday, December 29, 2011 @ 9:10 AM

A burning desire,
If one can't have it, what then?
Move on with your life

Wednesday, December 28, 2011 @ 10:30 AM

Writing in drama,
The screaming and the pointing,
All he wants is peace

Thursday, December 22, 2011 @ 6:37 PM

Dwindling faith and hope.
He is ready for you, Lord,
His job is done here

Sunday, October 16, 2011 @ 9:13 pm

It is dark outside,
They keep running and running,
Soon, the sun will shine

Tuesday, October 18, 2011 @ 7:58 am

The still of the night,
His mind is strong, thoughts are clear,
Creating his prose

Wednesday, October 19, 2011 @ 3:19 am

Running in the dark,
Under canopy of trees,
Hugged by morning fog

Sunday, October 23, 2011 @ 11:26 am

Morning dew glistens,
new week, new day, a new start,
Holding on to hope

Monday, October 24, 2011 @ 7:57 am

Shadows crossing paths,
A medley of silhouettes,
Runners and walkers

Wednesday, October 26, 2011 @ 6:02 am

A runner's chorus,
A winded greeting echoes,
"Mornin'" - "Good morning!"

Wednesday, October 26, 2011 @ 6:02 am

He wakes before dawn,
Creative juices flowing,
Producing new art

Friday, October 28, 2011 @ 6:50 am

He reminisces,
Reliving days of his youth,
Lives every moment

Friday, November 4, 2011 @ 4:26 am

Reliving their youth,
Like little boys, they create,
New music, new art

Saturday, October 29, 2011 @ 6:38 am

Your love is boundless,
Loving, patient, gentle, kind,
Deep humility

Tuesday, November 29, 2011 @ 10:20 PM

Buying time to breathe,
Wheels in motion for a chance,
Hope for the better

Monday, October 31, 2011 @ 8:01 pm

Harnessing his dog,
Together they run in stride,
Peaceful and tranquil

Wednesday, November 2, 2011 @ 9:12 am

His mind races,
Thinking of all his deeds,
Justifying

Friday, November 4, 2011 @ 4:26 am

60

Seeking inner peace,
Mother Nature's beauty heals,
Peace comes from within

Wed., Nov. 16, 2011 @ 7:37 PM

He longs for his home,
Anticipating his flight,
Awaiting landing

Sunday, November 6, 2011 @ 7:11 am

Colors are vivid,
Lapping water, cool breezes,
Natural beauty

Wed., Nov. 16, 2011 @ 7:37 PM

She kisses my face,
Feel her natural beauty,
Caressing my soul

Thurs., Nov. 17, 2011 @ 8:13 PM

62

Finding happiness,
external or internal,
It comes from within

Fri., Nov. 18, 2011 @ 2:36 PM

Potpourri of life,
Like the ocean, far and wide,
Wonderland of life

Friday, November 25, 2011 @ 10:58 PM (revised 2/1/13)

Food and family,
Gathering and giving thanks,
Counting our blessings

Thursday, November 24, 2011 @ 4:47 PM

She calls from afar,
She talks to me through her songs,
Pleading my return

Saturday, November 20, 2011 @ 12:00 PM

No need for drama,
Be calm, cool and collected,
And, just keep smiling

Saturday, November 26, 2011 @ 1:09 PM

His body's aching,
Master of his mind, push on,
He trudges forward

Sat., Nov. 19, 2011 @ 10:07 PM

Apprehensive choice,
Cornered, looking for an out,
A resolution

Monday, October 31, 2011 @ 8:01 pm

Just me and nature,
Explore wonder and beauty,
Pure tranquility

Tuesday, November 1, 2011 @ 10:42 pm

Molting like a fowl,
Greens, browns, yellows, you're changing,
Carpeting the ground

Wednesday, November 30, 2011 @ 10:27 AM

Honoring Mary,
Immaculate Conception,
God bless Mater Dei

Wednesday, December 7, 2011 @ 10:45 PM

You gave us your son,
Still, others ridiculed you,
The Mother of God

Thursday, December 8, 2011 @ 7:30 AM

Relations can hurt,
Jesus' love reminds us,
Love and forgiveness

Friday, December 9, 2011 @ 7:56 AM

You've given me hope,
You've loved me, inspired me,
You've won me over

Monday, December 12, 2011 @ 8:04 AM

Running in the rain,
With Koa, my protector,
Just one of my loves

Monday, December 12, 2011 @ 8:04 AM

The Raincoat Runner,
Eliminates the excuse,
Continues his quest

Tuesday, December 13, 2011 @ 8:09 AM

The brisk Winter air,
Gnaws at my clothes and my skin,
I just keep running

Friday, December 16, 2011 @ 8:22 AM

His self-discipline,
Guides him closer to his goal,
Determination

Tuesday, December 27, 2011 2@ 8:51 AM

Suicide Hill run,
Birds are quiet, trees are still,
Mission accomplished

Thursday, November 24, 2011 @ 4:47 PM

Determination,
He's committed to his health,
Repertoire is set

Monday, December 19, 2011 @ 10:48 AM

What is a true friend,
No conditions with God's love,
It's reciprocal

Wednesday, December 14, 2011 @ 8:37 AM

God does work wonders,
Keep life simple and humble,
His love is boundless

Saturday, December 17, 2011 @ 9:05 AM

He gave us His gift,
Unto us a child was born,
We named him Matthew

Tuesday, December 20, 2011 @ 10:15 AM

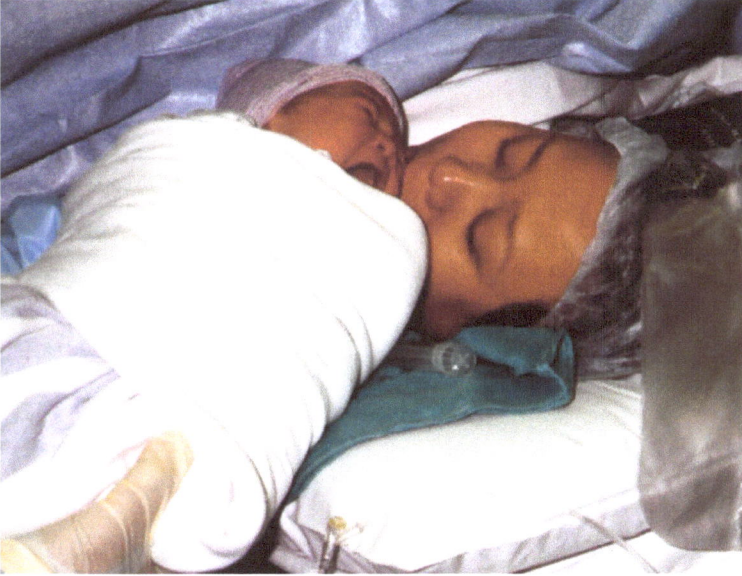

Know a mother's love,
For nine months to a lifetime,
Her love never ends

Wednesday, December 21, 2011 @ 9:15 AM

Angels in disguise,
He sends them at the right time,
Sends His love through them

Friday, December 23, 2011 @ 9:42 AM

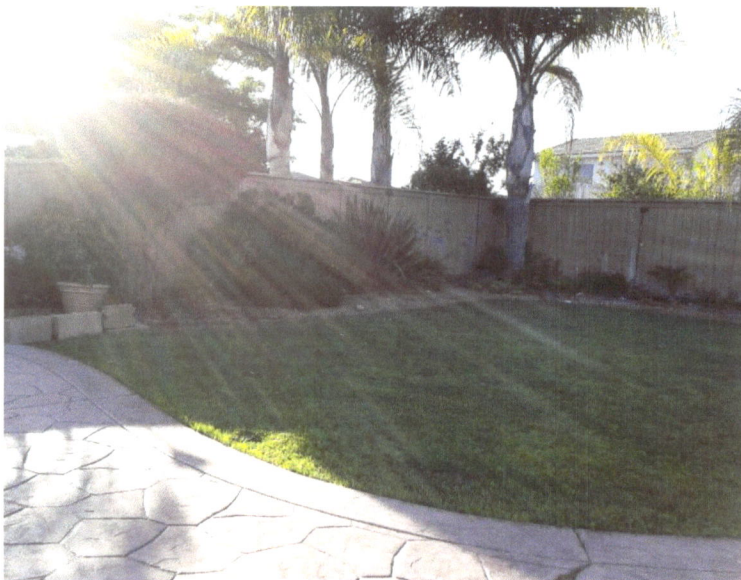

Hustle and bustle,
Shopping, school plays, church, parties,
The Season's reason?

Tuesday, December 6, 2011 @ 5:02 PM

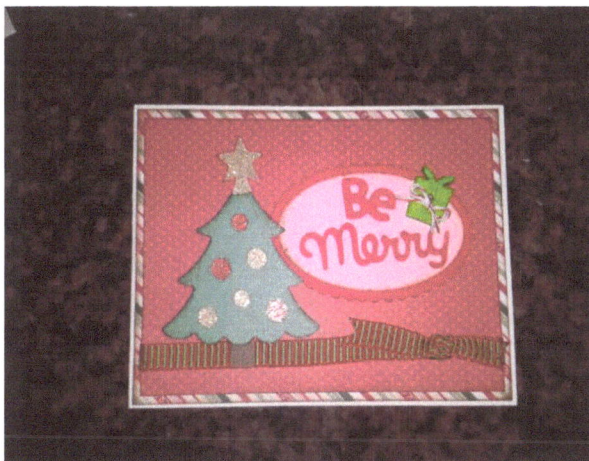

Spirit of Christmas,
Filling hearts and homes with joy,
Share the gift of love

(Greeting card created by Regina B. Yagyagan)
Friday, December 23, 2011 @ 9:42 AM

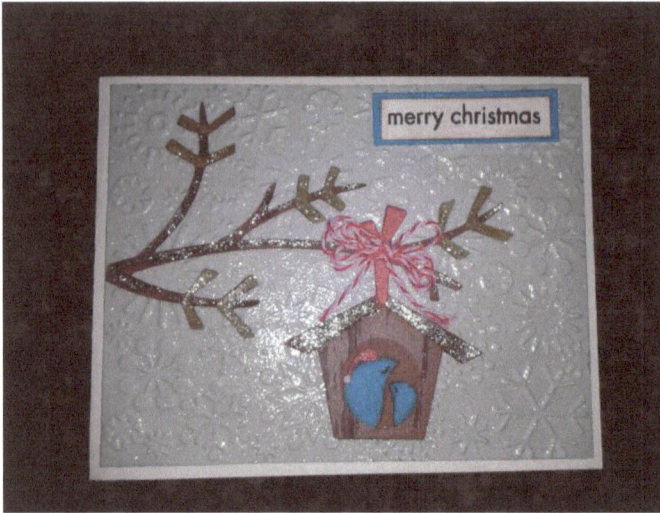

Christmas aloha,
Tropical flowers, tradewinds,
Live the simple life

(Greeting card created by Regina B. Yagyagan)
Monday, November 28, 2011 @ 10:45 PM

Find the connection,
Truth, love and sincerity,
We're a family

(Greeting card created by Regina B. Yagyagan)
Monday, December 26, 2011 @ 10:00 AM

Define family,
Love unconditionally,
We have become one.

Saturday, October 22, 2011 @ 7:01 am

Life's simple moments,
Spending time with our loved ones,
Money can't buy it

(L to R: Regina, Matthew, Gabrielle and Steve Yagyagan)
Saturday, December 31, 2011 @ 8:12 PM

Thank you for reading my first book of haiku poems. I hope you enjoyed it. Tell your friends and family. Again, I hope my poems and photographs touch your life in some positive way. Feel free to e-mail me with feedback at

plantationprince@gmail.com

and visit my blog:

www.PrinceofthePlantation.blogspot.com

for updates on my books. Remember, **Live, love and laugh with PASSION!**

Aloha,
Steve